ISBN 0-87666-996-8

Inside Front Cover:
In the wild, peach-faced lovebirds, *Agapornis roseicollis,* live in comparatively small groups, mostly in areas that are dry and grow leaf-shedding trees, though they are usually in the vicinity of a body of water.

Inside Back Cover:
The golden-shouldered parakeet, *Psephotus c. chrysopterygius,* is a very rare species in the wild and seems to be confined to the western shores of Cape York Peninsula and the coast of the southeast part of the Gulf of Carpenteria. Immature birds are like females except for the bright blue cheek patches of the male.

Title Page:
The Indian ringneck parakeet, *Psittacula krameri manillensis,* is one of the loveliest of all the larger parakeets. The graceful and slender proportions of the birds seem to be in perfect harmony with their simple design and pastel colors.

Distributed in the U.S. by T.F.H. Publications, Inc., 211 West Sylvania Avenue, P.O. Box 427, Neptune, N.J. 07753; in England by T.F.H. (Gt. Britain) Ltd., 13 Nutley Lane, Reigate, Surrey; in Canada to the book store and library trade by Beaverbooks, 953 Dillingham Road, Pickering, Ontario L1W 1Z7; in Canada to the pet trade by Rolf C. Hagen Ltd., 3225 Sartelon Street, Montreal 382, Quebec; in Southeast Asia by Y.W. Ong, 9 Lorong 36 Geylang, Singapore 14; in Australia and the South Pacific by Pet Imports Pty. Ltd., P.O. Box 149, Brookvale 2100, N.S.W., Australia; in South Africa by Valiant Publishers (Pty.) Ltd., P.O. Box 78236, Sandton City, 2146, South Africa; Published by T.F.H. Publications, Inc., Ltd., The British Crown Colony of Hong Kong.

DWARF PARROTS

Dr. Matthew M. Vriends
and
Petra Bleher

1 3 2

4

1. *The Barnard's parakeet, Platycercus* or *Barnardius zonarius barnardi*, is also known as the mallee ringneck parakeet. It is one of the most popular birds in aviculture. 2. The Cloncurry parakeet, *P.* or *B. z. macgillivrayi*, is very rare in the wild (intericr of central Queensland). 3. In captivity parrots and parakeets are easily fed and will remain in excellent condition on a relatively simple diet. The fact that a diet is simple does not mean that nutrition need not be all-inclusive. 4. The sun conure, *Aratinga solstitialis*, is one of the most striking of all conures.

The mulga parrot, *Psephotus varius*, or many-color parakeet, is a high-class cousin of the popular and charming redrump parakeet and more diversified in color.

Hanging parrots (genus *Loriculus*) are close relatives of the lovebirds. Their name derives from the fact that they hang upside down in their roosts.

Introduction

More than 200 years ago, a Swedish botanist named Carl von Linne (the oft-published Latinized version of which is Carolus Linnaeus) took the first steps toward a standardized system of nomenclature of all living things. Basically what Linnaeus did was to give everything known to him at least a first and second name. Thus he dispensed with common names that differed from one region to another and substituted scientific names (usually derived from Latin or Greek), hoping that every scientist would be able to accept his system of binominial nomenclature and thus end the uncertainty which resulted when someone in Sweden would read about a certain bird written by a Frenchman, for example.

The orange-fronted conure, *Aratinga canicularis*, shown above, resembles the peach-fronted conure, *Aratinga aurea*, shown to the left. Some of the aratingas' common characteristics are the long, slender shape, long tapering tail, large head, and large beak. Conures are like miniature macaws.

This story relates to the title of our book. "Dwarf parrots" is not a scientific name. As a matter of fact there is no scientific grouping which recognizes the size of a bird as that characteristic which is important enough to make it a "natural" group. The same is true, by the way, for almost all other animals including fishes, mammals, etc. We therefore have to define what we mean by "dwarf parrots," and that definition will be valid only for this book. From an avicultural point of view we'll consider as a "dwarf parrot" any bird small enough to be kept in a portable cage which can easily be carried by the average person. We also shall limit the species we cover mainly to those with pointed tails (versus the square tails of the usually larger parrots). Other authors usually refer to this group as "parakeets," and the only reason we prefer not to use this as a title to this book is because in the United States "parakeet" is usually utilized as a name for the Australian shell parakeet, or the budgerigar as it is known in England and the rest of the English-speaking world.

To get back to Linnaeus, his names of living things were written so that the genus name (what we might consider our family surname) came first. Thus according to his system his name might have been Linnaeus Carolus and his son might have been Linnaeus Johannus, so to speak. Many peoples of the world (Chinese, Malay, etc.) utilize a system in which their family name comes first. For our small parrots, or parakeets, we have certain groups (genera) which fall into the previously defined category and which we shall designate using both their scientific names and their popular names. We are indebted to the book *Parrots of the World* by Forshaw and Cooper, the 1978 edition published by T.F.H. Publications, Inc., for the identifications. There is still a lot of controversy and changing of names going on in the parrot world, and it is really a matter of choice which authority to follow. Since Forshaw and Cooper's book is the most recent and most complete (every species of parrot illustrated with a color drawing) . . . and since it is also the most available . . . we have followed it as a guide.

In the scientific descriptions of the various parakeets covered by this book, you will encounter birds that are so closely related that, except for very small differences, they are identical. These closely related but slightly different birds are called "subspecies," since they are not sufficiently different from their brethren to be listed as a separate species. This will be much clearer when you read about the subspecies later on in this book.

WHAT IS A PARAKEET OR DWARF PARROT?

There are about 8,700 different living species of birds in the world. This is a mere fraction of the many species which have appeared since the world had its first bird inhabitant some 150,000,000 years ago. Fortunately, man cannot be blamed for the extinction of so many species, though he is doing his best to kill what is left by destroying their natural habitat and shooting them. The only hope is to import them from the wilds and put them into the hands of skilled aviculturists who will breed them. The "profit motive" is the only logical basis upon which to hope that many of the rare parrots will be saved. Encourage people to breed them by making them valuable, and people like you will try. Not only for the money . . . but to be the first person to breed a species in captivity. The hungry native in the jungle considers parrots as little more than food . . . or a nuisance that eats his crops . . . or a screaming mob that wakes him up in the morning . . . or a source of feathers. But no one can reach him (physically or mentally) to tell him to "preserve this endangered species." In March 1979, Dr. Herbert R. Axelrod attended a meeting sponsored by the United Nations dealing with the problem of endangered species. There is no simple solution, but his proposal that rare birds be bred in captivity was accepted as the

1 and 2. The orange-fronted conure, *Aratinga canicularis canicularis*, inhabits the Pacific slopes of Central America. 3. The cactus conure, *A. c. cactorum*, comes from Brazil. 4. The red-vented parakeet, *Pionus menstruus*, is from tropical South America and is reasonably expensive. 5. The orange-chinned parakeet, *Brotogeris jugularis*, ranges from southern Mexico through central South America.

1

2

3

4

5

15

only sensible approach, thus opening the door for the importation of many species which were not previously available. Only Australia persisted in preferring to allow their farmers to shoot birds down rather than to allow them to be exported.

Birds are in the class Aves. This class is a section of the vertebrate animals (animals with backbones). The class Aves itself is broken into subcategories known as orders, and one of these orders is the parrots. The scientific name of the order of parrots is Psittaciformes. This order is further broken down into families, genera, species and subspecies. But a parrot would be defined by its obvious characteristics. All parrots have feathers and have a "parrot-like beak." This beak or bill is round (as contrasted to pointed, as in a canary), short and narrow, with the top part curved over the bottom part and fitting nicely over it; the upper mandible is hinged movably to the skull. The toes are also characteristic (though other birds, such as woodpeckers, also have the same kind of toes). Parrots have four toes. The center two toes point forward, while the first and fourth toes point backwards. The feet of most parrots are used for grasping and climbing; the bill is used for the same purposes as well as for feeding and defense. Parrots have other interesting characteristics that—taken in combination—make them different from other birds. Their heads are large when compared to the rest of their bodies (think of canaries' heads, for example), and their necks are short; also they have huge, fleshy tongues) which, like humans', can be manipulated to hold food particles. They also have special organs which release powder; these organs are scattered among their feathers. That's what parrots are . . . but you can recognize them primarily by their hooked bills, though there are a few other birds with hooked bills that are not parrots (think of owls, eagles, falcons and the like!).

PHYSICAL PARTS OF THE DWARF PARROTS

All dwarf parrots, parakeets, budgerigars, cockatiels, macaws . . . every member of the order Psittaciformes . . . are called parrots. Aside from the special features mentioned above which differentiate parrots from other birds, there are many physical features of dwarf parrots which we must discuss in order for you to have a clear understanding of what physical characteristics are of importance in parrot keeping.

FEATHERS

Obviously parrots have feathers. Feathers, taken as a whole, are called plumage. The various feathers are grouped according to their functions and are given names. The feathers growing out of the head, such as those found in cockatiels and cockatoos, are called the crest. The wings have very specialized feathers. Those feathers which merely cover the fleshy part of the wing are called just that, covers. But scientists prefer to use the French word for covers: *coverts*. The small coverts which start as shingles on the edge of the wing that hits the air when the parrot flies are called the lesser wing coverts because they are the smallest feathers. These are followed by slightly larger wing feathers called median wing coverts, and the larger coverts (still covering the flesh of the wing itself) are called secondary coverts. The outside edge of the wing has the primary coverts, which are the largest coverts of them all. Basically coverts, then, are differentiated by the size of the feathers. Those feathers which extend beyond the flesh of the wing and are used for flying are usually called flights, though they often are called primary and secondary flights. Parrots need only their primary flights to fly. You can pluck them bald, but if you leave on their flights they can fly. On the other hand, if they have all their feathers except their flights, they cannot fly. Thus, newly acquired birds

1

1. White-eared conures, *Pyrrhura leucotis*, are quite rare in captivity. 2. The maroon-bellied conure, *Pyrrhura frontalis*, has a large range that extends from southern Brazil into Argentina. 3. Right: the pearly conure, *Pyrrhura perlata*, from northeastern Brazil. Left: the white-eared conure is one of the most attractive members of its genus.

2

3

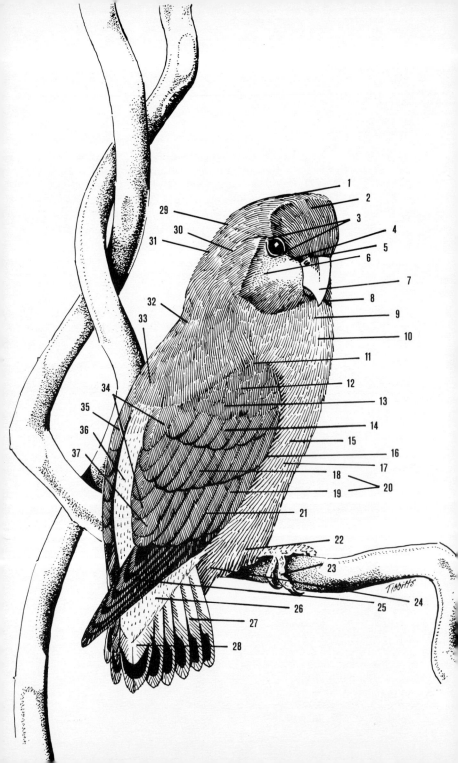

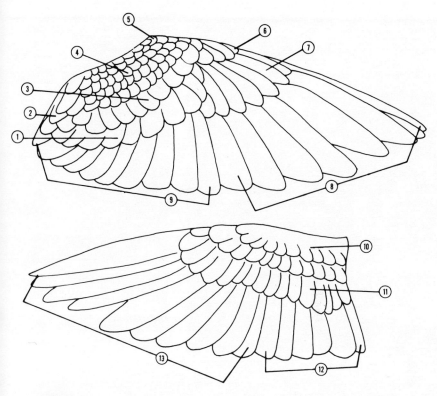

WING
1. secondary-coverts. 2. tertials. 3. median wing-coverts. 4. lesser wing-coverts. 5. bend of wing. 6. carpal edge. 7. primary coverts. 8. primaries. 9. secondaries. 10. lesser under wing coverts. 11. greater under wing coverts. 12. secondaries. 13. primaries.

TOPOGRAPHY OF A BIRD
1. crown. 2. forehead. 3. periophthalmic ring and region. 4. lores. 5. cere. 6. cheek. 7. upper mandible. 8. chin. 9. throat. 10. foreneck. 11. bend of wing. 12 upper wing. 13 lesser wing coverts. 14. media wing coverts. 15. breast. 15. carpal edge. 17. abdomen. 18. secondary coverts. 19. primary coverts. 20. greater wing coverts. 21. secondaries. 22. thigh (tibia). 23. foot. 24. under tail-coverts. 25. primaries. 26. upper tail-coverts. 27. lateral tail-coverts. 28. central tail-feathers. 29. nape. 30. ear coverts. 31. hindneck. 32 mantle. 33. upper back. 34, 35, 37. tertials. 36. rump.

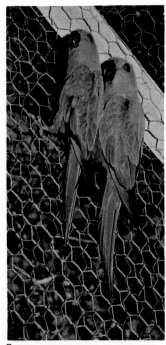

4

(1, 2, 3) The jendaya conure, *Aratinga jandaya,* is one of the favorites in the large family of conures. The vivid and vibrant beauty of this bird is dimmed only by its loud and raucous voice, a disadvantage in some environments. 4. The nanday conure, *Nandayus nenday,* has an attractive color scheme that shows up best in the company of the brighter and better known jendaya conure.

may often have the flights cut on one wing to keep the bird from flying. How often have I visited a jungle town in Africa or South America to be greeted by a native with a few small parrots on a stick offering them for sale. "See how tame they are," he would say. "They don't even fly away!" But ask him to hold the parrot in his hand and you'll see how wild they are. The only reason the bird stays on the stick is because it has had its flight feathers plucked or cut and cannot fly.

Besides the location of the feathers on the body, there are different kinds of feathers which are differentiated according to their construction. *Contour feathers* include flights and coverts and are usually visible. Down feathers are the soft, fluffy feathers which are so great for pillows. These are usually under the coverts and are usually invisible, as they act as insulation and are loosely held in the skin of the parrot. Parrots and some other birds have special feathers called *powder down feathers.* The powder down feather is a modified down feather which has barbs which decompose into a powder. The birds use this powder for cleaning themselves. It gives the other feathers a groomed, glossy look. Once you are able to hold and fondle your own parakeet, you might feel a powdery substance that has been deposited on your hands in the process. This powdery substance is a product of the powder down feathers.

When your dwarf parrots shed or lose a feather, you might care to save it. Use it as a book marker, or study its elegant color pattern if it hapens to be a colorful feather.

One term which is not "normal" in terms of parts of a parrot is the feather called a *"blood feather."* During the process of clipping a bird's flight feathers to restrict the bird's ability to fly, the base of the feather is usually left in. This shaft hinders the growth of a new feather, thus maintaining the parrot in a flightless condition for an extended period of time. Sometimes, for one reason or another, these shafts fill with blood, and should the bird damage them it might well bleed to death. These *blood feathers,* then, are shafts of cut feathers which have filled with blood. They are dangerous; if you notice any blood feathers on your parrot, you should have them removed by a veterinarian experienced in dealing with birds or by the person from whom you acquired your parakeet.

COLOR

The color of a parrot is determined genetically, and when two birds are similar in most respects except for some color differences, they are usually considered a subspecies. Thus color is helpful in the scientific determination of the species. The cause of the colors in parrots' feathers is quite complex, but it is similar to the same pigments found in fishes and snakes, and these pigments may mix to form other colors. Purple, for example, is usually a mixture of blue and red pigments.

Color alone is unimportant as a factor in assessing the health of a bird. Some subspecies may be more or less colorful, and it has nothing to do with one bird being healthier than the other. You usually can assist the bird in having bright colors by color feeding. Color feeding is the process of feeding a bird special foods to enhance its color. While parrots are not usually color-fed, canaries and flamingos must be fed special carotene-rich foods (paprika, shrimp, etc.) to enhance the red coloration or the birds will become white instead of the rich pink. The same may be true for certain parrots, but the authors have not had any personal experience with color-feeding parakeets, though white parrots have been dyed pink and bright red on many occasions and offered for sale as "something new!"

SKULL AND HEAD

The skull contains the brain. The head contains the skull,

(1, 2, 3) The Quaker parakeet, *Myiopsitta monachus,* is a very free breeder and a pleasant aviary inhabitant. This parakeet is one of the few specimens of parrots which builds a nest. The nest itself may be a gigantic affair composed of large and small twigs, grasses, and anything else at hand.

2

3

eyes, cere, bill, tongue, etc. It might well be that parrots have larger brains than most other birds when the weight of the brain is expressed as a percentage of total body weight. For this reason they are easily trainable and mimic so well. The only problem with this hypothesis is that it has been shown that the smaller parrots have relatively larger brains than the larger parrots!! Yet larger parrots are easier to tame and train to talk and act.

TONGUE

Parrots have very special tongues. They are thick and fleshy, and if you hand a parakeet a seed you will see his tongue come into action in holding the seed before he closes his bill on your helpful fingers! The tip of a parrot's tongue may well be hardened or callused. In the brush-tongued species (the lories, for example) the tip of the tongue is equipped with brush-like ends that facilitate the collection of pollen.

BILLS

A parrot's bill or beak is its trademark. How many people have been called "parrot-nose?" What is so special about a parrot's beak is that both the top and bottom are hinged and can be moved quite independently of each other. One of the ancient questions about parrots is this: It is universally agreed that the shape of a parrot's beak is ideal for cracking nuts and opening seeds, but why should such a wonderful natural tool be wasted on brush-tongued species that eat only pollen? Or on the grass parakeets, which feed only on soft seeds found on the ground? Or on those parrots which only eat the soft flesh of fruits? The answer usually given (never to our satisfaction) is that the feeding function is only one function of the bill. Its main function might well be to help the bird climb, build a nest and defend itself, and it may need that strong bill to tear off a bit of fruit and carry it away to chew it in its own time and convenience.

THE GUT

The gut or digestive tract is about the same to be found in all other birds. Think of it as a long tube which starts at the mouth and ends at the anus. Special organs called "crops" and "gizzards" occur in birds. The crop is the place where the food is stored and processed before being passed to the gizzard. The gizzard stores gravel and stones which help break the cellulose covering of seeds, thus making them digestible. Most birds require gravel, sand or something hard to help them break up the seeds. Most birds which feed their young produce a "milk" which is often called "pigeon's milk." This is a milky exudate produced in the gut which is regurgitated to feed youngsters.

PARROTS IN THEIR NATIVE LANDS

The dwarf parrots, or parakeets, which we are discussing in this book are found in Africa, South and Central America, Australia and the Pacific up to southeast Asia (Sri Lanka and India). Many parrots have been liberated in Europe, the United States, Hong Kong and other areas in order to establish them as local populations. The great English experiment was doomed to disaster by the hunters. Florida was a very successful habitat for many tropical birds, as was Hong Kong and Singapore, especially for the Indian Ringnecks.

Generally speaking, parrots are very difficult to observe at close range in their natural habitat. Throughout the jungles of the world, you can see them flying high over the jungle floor, usually in pairs. More often than not, they are screaming a familiar cry as they go by. South American parrots are usually collected by professionals who rob the nests

Left: The canary-winged parakeet, *Brotogeris versicolorus chiriri,* one of the twenty-two members of the genus *Brotogeris* that make southern Mexico through central South America their home. Above: The Princess parrot, *Polytelis alexandrae,* a rare bird in captivity, and rather expensive. It is very peaceful with other congenial birds.

of the developing young, hand-feed them and sell them to petshops. These birds are ideal because they are so well conditioned, healthy and tame. The parrot babies have about a 95% chance of survival when they are collected and cared for this way. Wild parrots left to grow up in nature have about a 12% chance for survival.

African parrots, unfortunately, are quite a different story. Most of them arrive after having been collected in the wild. Their flight feathers have been chopped off (hacked off would be a better term), and it is not unusual to see a chunk of the meat of the wing, bones and all, also hacked off. The birds are usually in frightful condition and require weeks of conditioning before they should even be considered as housepets.

Most parakeets and dwarf parrots sold in pet shops are domesticated. These are raised in huge quantities in South Africa or America and shipped all over the world. You can almost always tell a wild bird from a domesticated one by the seamless aluminum band on the foot of the baby. Usually this band must be put on when the chick is between one and two weeks old. After that it is too old and the foot is too large. Not all breeders put on seamless leg bands . . . but if they do, you have a breeder who cares!

In most of the cases when parrots range near a native village, you will find that the natives have domesticated a few birds and use them as housepets. Even "wild, savage" Indians from Brazil have been found to be pet-lovers. They keep the birds as a source of friendship and feathers. Feathers are the most colorful natural objects available to Indians. They don't rot, fade or smell.

Parrots probably originated in the land mass that now occupies the position of Antarctica and ranged into Australia and South America. Most are found south of the equator. Australia, New Guinea and the surrounding area have more than 100 of the 332 species of parrots known to still exist in the world. Africa has 24. Brazil, Colombia, and

Venezuela have 167 species. Mexico has 18 species and Argentina has 25 species. Of course some species have extended ranges which cross political boundaries, but other species may be isolated in a small ecological niche and occur on only one small island.

While some parrots (the kea from New Zealand, for example) enjoy the snow, most prefer the tropics. So keep your parakeet at room temperature. It doesn't matter how cold it gets at night (within reason) as long as your parrot can climb into a small cave-like box and stay warm. The bird's down feathers will see to that.

Depending upon the species, your parrot will either be a ground-loving, seed-eating bird (like the grass parakeets), or it might well like ripe fruits. When you buy the bird ascertain what its previous owner fed it and continue the same diet. It doesn't make much sense to try to duplicate the parrot's original diet in its natural habitat if you can find an acceptable substitute. But you should remember that there is a big difference between a bird eating seeds and fruits from a living plant and a bird eating dried, possibly dead seeds and dried fruits you might offer it. For this reason an extensive method of testing seeds for germination is presented in the appropriate section further on in the book.

BREEDING PARROTS

Breeding certain parrots is easy. It certainly takes little effort to breed budgerigars, cockatiels, lovebirds, grass parakeets and the like. But breeding lories is something else! Undoubtedly, every species of parrot can be bred in captivity. Even the huge macaws breed regularly if they are properly managed. If you ever have the chance to visit the Parrot Jungle in Miami, Florida or the Jurong Bird Farm in Singapore, or Walsrode, Germany, where perhaps the most exotic collection of birds is to be found, you'll have some idea of how relatively simple it is to breed parrots . . . provided you have the space and environment!

For the beginner, the major problem is getting a pair. In the Parrot Jungle, for example, they may have ten hyacinth macaws. They merely put them together in a huge cage and allow them to pair off by themselves. It is not that easy for you. As a matter of fact, it's fairly difficult to even sex most of the parrots ... and then, too, just putting a male and female together doesn't always result in breeding.

If you are seriously interested in breeding your parrots, here are a few tips. Most parrots (but not the snow-loving kea) mate for life and are monogamous. If you find a species which interests you and which you find simple to maintain, then acquire as many specimens as possible. The usual number to insure success is five. If you can find five members of the same species which are mature enough (about two years old in most cases, though younger for the smaller species), your chances of getting a pair are almost certain (32 to 1). The problem is verifying their age, as many larger birds have an adult plumage even though they are not sexually mature. With budgerigars the color of the cere (nostrils) alone is usually enough, and they are so small and inexpensive that their care is simple even if you do have five to care for.

Most Amazons can breed before they are three years old, and it is probably safe to say that birds as large (or small) as Amazons or rosellas (*Platycercus*) and such related genera as *Barnardius, Cyanoramphus, Psephotus* and *Neophema* all mature within 24-36 months after birth. Smaller birds mature their first year and larger birds mature their fourth year.

NESTS

Most parrots are cave brooders. They require a hole in the ground or a hole in a tree. This is successfully imitated by the wooden nest box which is available at most pet shops. This is merely a wooden box with a hole large enough for the bird to enter. Under the hole is a peg upon which the bird lands prior to entering the box. The bottom of the nest box may have a rounded, concave platform to keep the eggs from rolling into an inaccessible corner away from a brooding hen. With the larger parrots, a wooden anything is short-lived. The parrots simply tear it apart. In this case you have to use metal; a trash can serves well if you simply cut a hole in it for an entrance. All nest boxes should have an access from outside the cage so you can look in when you become curious to see how things are developing. Most parakeets do not add anything to the nest. They merely lay their eggs on the bottom. But after continued use the bottom becomes lined with hardened droppings. There is considerable difference of opinion about the acceptability of these accumulated droppings. If these droppings are not infested with insects, leave them alone. If they harbor vermin, then clean them out.

COURTSHIP

Unlike pigeons, chickens, peacocks and certain other highly social birds, parrots have a very weak and limited courtship procedure. They may have some movements of the wings and feathers, accompanied by eye dilations, but it is usually over with very quickly. They usually don't even sing each other a song! This is probably due to their monogamous life. Most courtship rituals, including songs and special breeding colors, are nature's way of helping breeding birds find and recognize each other. With parrots and their high intelligence, this may not be necessary.

EGGLAYING AND INCUBATION

Parrots all lay white eggs. The eggs are relatively small, as are the eggs of most other species that feed their young.

The number of eggs varies with the species, but in general parrots have from two to eight eggs laid between 24 and 48 hours apart.

The parents usually start to incubate the eggs (sit on them) after the second egg is laid, but this varies widely even in the same species. Hatching may take place from two to five weeks after incubation takes place. In some species only the female sits, and in this case she is fed by the male. In other cases both species sit.

At birth the chicks of all parrots are blind and naked. They soon develop a soft down for insulation. The color of the down may vary from species to species and from diet to diet. Within two weeks the eyes usually open; at this time the male may start feeding the chicks directly. Up to this time the male usually feeds the female, and she then feeds herself and the chicks. Most of the small parrots we are interested in here remain in the nest box for about one month, though large macaws may stay in the nest box for a whole season (3-4 months).

With some species, especially domesticated budgerigars, cockatiels and lovebirds, it is possible that the breeders might start another nest while the young of the previous brood still come and go in their original nest box. When this happens there is bound to be trouble for the chicks. Remove them immediately if you suspect the hen is preparing another nest. This is usually indicated by her spending an inordinate amount of time in the nest box.

FOSTER PARENTS

There are many, many cases of egg-switching. One of the authors has always used pigeons to incubate the eggs of his parrots. When the pigeons have hatched the eggs they successfully feed the babies, as some of the fancy pigeon varieties have short beaks. It is also possible to put various eggs under different species of parrots. However, foster incubating is rarely done as compared to foster feeding.

The foster parents may suddenly stop feeding their foster chicks because they sense something is wrong. If this happens, you must be prepared to feed the chicks yourself. This is hard, hard work, for many parakeet chicks require constant feeding every hour or two. If you have a nest of 5 chicks, this means a 24 hour per day job for a week. But it gradually requires less and less time as the chicks grow up, and the rewards are great. When you have successfully hand-fed a few birds, they consider you their mother and father! They are so tame and friendly . . . and trainable . . . that many aviculturists actually hand-feed certain birds just to develop this strong relationship.

THEIR FIRST FEATHERS

Juvenile birds look anything but beautiful as they develop their first coat of feathers. Their plumage is usually rough, spotty, lackluster and sparse. The coloration is usually that of the female (for camouflage purposes probably). The process of molting is when birds lose their feathers and have been replaced with new ones. This is usually an annual event after the first year. Of course, during the first year the birds first lose their down and then their juvenile feathers and then get their first mature plumage. Birds require special attention during their molting periods, as the construction of feathers requires a well balanced diet.

FEEDING YOUR PARROT

As previously mentioned, parrots have certain basic requirements which may include fruits, seeds, greens, cuttlebone, sand, gravel, charcoal and woods upon which to chew. Since they spend most of their time in fruit or nut trees, it is safe to offer them branches of fruit and nut trees to chew upon . . . leaves, branches and all. Just be sure that you have carefully and thoroughly washed the branches and leaves in running water (a garden hose or in your shower) to rid them of all traces of insecticides or chemical fertilizers.

If your parrot doesn't like what you offer it, don't be discouraged. Parrots sometimes take a few days to get accustomed to a certain food. Obviously, you cannot offer a hard-shelled nut to a small parakeet, because its bill isn't strong enough or big enough to crack the shell. (Don't offer walnuts to budgies!) But most parrots love peanuts and sunflower seeds, especially if they are shelled! They also like to have a slice of an orange, a piece of ripe banana or just about any other tropical fruit that is soft and ripe.

For sanitary reasons only, remove the fruit after the first day (before the first night), otherwise you might become invaded with fruitflies. Fortunately, fruitflies don't bite people or birds, and they quickly die if you remove the fruit. Besides the dried seeds we get at the pet shop, we often give our caged parakeets the advantage of sprouted seeds. This also tests the quality of the seed you are buying. If the seed you buy is dead and does not sprout, then it has very little food value. This is the big problem with seed purchased in supermarkets where price is the only consideration. "Dead" seed is half the price of "guaranteed to germinate" seed.

To get the seeds to sprout, merely take a few handfuls of seed just as it is mixed in the package you buy at your local pet shop. Soak the seed for three hours in room-temperature water. Use a fine strainer (the size used for rice is fine), put the seeds in the strainer and place the strainer in a glass bowl large enough to have the container (strainer) rest on the frame of the bowl. After the few hours of soaking, we run water over the seeds in the strainer (again, room temperature) for about five minutes. This removes the dirt loosened by the soaking process. Then we put them back into the same bowl and soak them for another twelve hours. After this soaking we give them another five-minute bath under running water. We then place them in shallow glass pans and add the moistened seed to a depth of about 5 to 6 cm (about 2 inches) and cover the top with a plastic or aluminum wrap. We place the pan on top of a refrigerator, where the temperature is usually warmer than the rest of the room. Within two days we notice that the seeds have sprouted, and we begin to feed them to our birds. Not all seeds sprout at the same time. We usually find that millet and canary seeds sprout together, but wheat, oat and sunflower seeds have a schedule of their own. Of course, if you are able to get individual seeds (unmixed), that will make life so much easier in terms of seed-sprouting. You can give your birds all they want of the sprouted seeds, but don't give them so much that it becomes foul.

You also can germinate (sprout) the seeds in a shallow pan of earth. Just plant the seeds in small aluminum trays with about two inches of dirt. When the seeds sprout, put the whole thing inside the cage and the parakeets will nibble on the grass or sprouts. The advantage of this sytem is that it's easier for you, but the birds then get only the grasses and not the roots and cotyledons (bases of the seeds).

Parakeets must be fed daily unless they are being trained. If you are training them, then they must be kept hungry and should be fed only when they associate the feeding with you. Try to feed them from your hand. In daily feeding, be sure that you are not fooled by the shells of the seed. Often beginners think their birds have not eaten because the seed cups are still full. This is not the case . . . the cups are merely full of shells that the birds drop in after they remove the seeds from inside the shells. Just blow into the seed cup and you'll realize what we mean. The particles that go flying out into the air are the shells, while those that remain are full seeds.

The small seedlings which develop after sprouting the seeds are a very good food for our birds. The small plants replace fresh greens; they are rich in the enzyme catalase and in vitamin A. This series of photos shows the sprouting of seeds from the first day to the tenth day exactly prepared as per the instructions on pages 38 and 39.

Preferably, the front of an aviary should face south. Obviously, a scenic spot with plants, bushes, flowers, etc. that can be seen from the house would be ideal.

Cages and Aviaries

Depending upon the species you wish to keep . . . and the number of birds of that species that you have . . . the size of the cage is up to you and your budget. Normally you should buy the largest cage you can afford. You should be concerned about the quality and size of the spacing of the wires so that the birds cannot slip through or chew their way out!

If you intend to breed your birds, get a cage easily cleaned and serviced from the outside. Then you don't have to disturb the parrots every time you want to clean their cage. You should clean the cage bottom, change the water, put in fresh seed and inspect the cage at least once a day. Of course, if you have multiple feeders, sufficient water and extra containers for grit (sand, charcoal), millet sprays, bits of fruit and leafy green vegetables and sprouts, you don't have to feed every day. But you should check, if for no other reason than to check the health of your bird(s).

If you are lucky enough to have a large basement or outdoor area that can be dedicated to bird keeping, you'll be able to set up an aviary. Aviaries really are simply large cages, usually made to order for the purposes of breeding a particular species. They have inside room for nest boxes, flight areas, mating areas, areas for bringing up the young, etc. By the time you become interested in breeding and in having an aviary setup you should have visited local bird breeders, joined a bird club and investigated what types of aviaries are successful for people in your own area. The temperature and climate in your area, and the species in which you are interested, determine the size and layout of your aviary. (The T.F.H. publication *Building An Aviary* provides excellent information, diagrams and photos.)

At the nestling stage parrot chicks (left) are amenable to handling and quickly become tame. In the breeding season the male plum-headed parakeet (right) shows a very amusing courtship. He spreads his wings slightly, draws his plumage close, and hops and bows around his bride.

The red-fronted conure,
Aratinga w. wagleri, (left)
and the blue-crowned con-
ure, *A. a. acuticauda* (right).

The Aymara parakeet,
Amoropsittaca aymara,
from Bolivia and Argentina
is a quiet, rather retiring
bird gentle enough to be
housed with several
smaller Australian
parakeets.

*Remarks
Referring
To The
Species*

GENUS *ARATINGA*

PEACH-FRONTED CONURE (*Aratinga aurea*)

Coloration: yellow-orange crown, bordered with blue. Eyes bordered with an orange band. Dark green neck and rump, the balance of the bird primarily light green with a yellowish green belly. Blue shades can be seen shining through in the wing feathers. Insides of the wings are light green to yellowish green. Eyes orange to brown. Beak and feet grayish black. Male and female are alike; youngsters similar to their parents although paler. The iris is gray.

Length: 28-29 cm, wings 14-15 cm, tail 13-14 cm.

Distribution: Brazil, eastern Bolivia and northern Paraguay and Argentina.

Subspecies: *Aratinga aurea aurea*

Coloration and Length: same as mentioned.

Distribution: the entire Amazon area, eastern Bolivia, Salta, northwestern Argentina.

Subspecies: *Aratinga aurea major*

Coloration and Length: as mentioned above.

Distribution: this subspecies lives in the vicinity of the Paraguay River in Paraguay and is so similar to the nominate race that it constantly confuses breeders and ornithologists.

This species populates preferably open and semi-open country. Its call is a raucous screech, especially when the birds are flying. Generally, a hollow tree serves nesting needs. The clutch consists of about six eggs, which are rounded. The peach-fronted conure is one of the most commonly imported species. Breeding successes have frequently been reported.

ORANGE-FRONTED CONURE
(*Aratinga canicularis*)

Coloration: mainly green; orange frontal band; crown blue; throat and breast pale olive green; abdomen, under tail-coverts and under wing-coverts light yellow; primaries green, blue towards the ends; outer webs of secondaries blue; tail green, below greenish-yellow; periophthalmic (eye) ring yellow. Young ones: similar but narrower frontal band; iris brown.

Length: 24 cm.

Distribution: western Central America—from Mexico to Costa Rica.

Subspecies:*Aratinga canicularis canicularis*

Coloration and length: as mentioned above.

Distribution: from Chiapas, southwestern Mexico, south to western Costa Rica.

Subspecies: *Aratinga canicularis eburnirostrum*
Coloration: In general as mentioned above, but the frontal band is smaller; underparts green; lower mandible with a brownish spot sidewise.
Length: similar.
Distribution: southwestern Mexico.

Subspecies: *Aratinga canicularis clarae*
Coloration: similar to that of *A.c. eburnirostrum,* although the frontal band is very small; blue crown continues down to lores; throat and breast green; lower mandible spot black.
Length: similar.
Distribution: western Mexico.

This species populates preferably deciduous forests with trees lining the water courses. The bird is a pretty bad screamer, but apart from that has a very pleasant nature and can be trained quickly, particularly if we buy young birds; older birds generally cannot be tamed and rarely become good talkers. Very often they use old woodpeckers' holes as nesting facilities. The clutch consists of three to five rounded eggs. The orange-fronted conure has been imported rarely.

CACTUS CONURE (*Aratinga cactorum*)
Coloration: green neck, back and rump. Brown-white forehead; bluish white crown. Grayish brown cheeks; light brown throat. Very obvious yellow stripe over the eye. Golden yellow breast, becoming darker toward the belly. Long pointed wings that are green with blue markings. The tail is also green with bluish green borders. Eyes yellow to brown; brownish gray beak and flesh-colored feet. Although it is not easy to determine the sex, a knowledge-

able fancier will not have that trouble, especially if he can compare the birds sitting next to each other. The female's coloring is less sharp.

Length: 25 cm.

Distribution: northeastern Brazil.

Subspecies: *Aratinga cactorum cactorum*
Coloration and length: as above mentioned.
Distribution: Bahia and Minas Gerais.

Subspecies: *Aratinga cactorum caixana*
Coloration: paler than mentioned above; throat and breast brownish; abdomen less orange, rather yellow.
Length and distribution: as mentioned under nominate race.

This species populates mostly inland areas, in small groups on the plains, in the thick underbrush, the high trees, or in high grass and weeds. Very little is known about their communication and breeding behavior in the wild. The eggs are broadly elliptical, and one clutch consists of about two to four eggs. They have been frequently imported, yet breeding successes are rarely reported.

BROWN-THROATED CONURE (*Aratinga pertinax*)

Coloration: Primarily green, with bright yellow forehead, cheeks and chin. Bluish black crown. Throat grayish brown, slowly changing to orange-yellow towards the belly. Clearly visible bluish black spot on the tail formed by four tail feathers attached at one point. Brown eyes, blackish gray beak and white cere; feet are gray-black to brown. The female is generally a little smaller in build (23-25 cm) and her coloring is also a little duller than the male's. Nevertheless, picking out a true pair can pose a few problems.

Length: 25 cm.

Distribution: Panama, northern South America and islands off the northern coast of Venezuela.

According to Forshaw there are 14 subspecies:

Subspecies: *Aratinga pertinax pertinax*

Coloration and length: as mentioned above.

Distribution: island of Curacao in the Netherlands Antilles, off the northern coast of Venezuela.

Subspecies: *Aratinga pertinax xanthogenia*

Coloration: almost like that of *A.p. pertinax,* yet the orange-yellow of the forehead continues to the crown.

Length: as nominate race.

Distribution: Only on the island of Bonaire in the Netherlands Antilles.

Subspecies: *Aratinga pertinax arubensis*

Coloration: basically as nominate race; orange-yellow restricted to periophthalmic region, more extensive below eye; forehead paler; greenish-blue of crown running to occiput; lores, cheeks and sides of head brownish and pale orange-yellow; ear-coverts yellow, edged with brown.

Length: as nominate race.

Distribution: Aruba.

Subspecies: *Aratinga pertinax aeruginosa*

Coloration: almost like that of *A.p. arubensis,* but with some yellow on forehead and around the eye; throat, breast and sides of head rather darker brown; crown coloration runs down to back and nape.

Length: mentioned above.

Distribution: northeastern Colombia.

Subspecies: *Aratinga pertinax lehmanni*

Coloration: like that of *A.p. aeruginosa,* but the orange-yellow eye area more developed; greenish blue only on fore-crown; tints of blue very much faded.

Length: mentioned above.

Distribution: eastern Colombia.

Subspecies: *Aratinga pertinax tortugensis*

Coloration: like that of *A.p. aeruginosa,* but more orange-yellow along the head, sides and throat, yet somewhat paler; under wing-coverts yellowish green.

Length: larger than nominate race.

Distribution: restricted to the Tortuga Islands.

Subspecies: *Aratinga pertinax margaritensis*

Coloration: forehead whitish; forecrown dull greenish blue; lores, cheeks and ear-coverts olive brown; periophthalmic orange-yellow; throat and upper breast pale olive.

Length: like nominate race.

Distribution: only on the Margarita and Los Frailes Islands.

Subspecies: *Aratinga pertinax venezuelae*

Coloration: like that of *A.p. margaritensis,* but paler yellowish on the back; tail feathers yellow-bordered; abdomen less orange.

Length: as mentioned in nominate race.

Distribution: throughout Venezuela with the exception of the northwestern section of the country.

Subspecies: *Aratinga pertinax chrysophrys*

Coloration: similar to that of *A.p. margaritensis,* but the brownish shades more obvious.

Length: like nominate race.

Distribution: Guyana, southeastern Venezuela and northern Brazil.

Subspecies: *Aratinga pertinax surinama*

Coloration: similar to that of *A.p. chrysophrys;* orange-yellow areas larger and brownish areas rather yellowish green.

Length: similar to nominate race.

Distribution: Guyana and Surinam and northeastern Venezuela.

Subspecies: *Aratinga pertinax chrysogenys*
Coloration: generally intensively darker shaded; outer flight feathers dark blue; abdomen with dark orange spots.
Length: like nominate race.
Distribution: not exactly defined, northwestern Brazil.

Subspecies: *Aratinga pertinax paraensis*
Coloration: upper parts dark green; under parts dark orange-yellow; forehead and crown bluish; outer webs of primaries and secondaries dark blue; throat, sides of head and breast brown; iris red.
Length: as nominate race.
Distribution: northern Brazil.

Subspecies: *Aratinga pertinax ocularis*
Coloration: ranging from pure green on crown and forehead to orange-yellow around the eye-area and running into a brownish shade on lores and head sides; paler yet on throat and upper breast; underparts yellow-green running into yellow towards abdomen. Young ones: much more greenish.
Length: as nominate race.
Distribution: The Pacific region of Panama.

This species usually populates the savannah regions of the above-mentioned countries referring to every subspecies. Their call is raucous and sharp during flight, always abruptly terminated. The females lay their eggs in natural crevices and holes in limestone rocks or in holes excavated in earthen banks or occasionally in tree holes. Their clutch usually consists of four to seven eggs, and more, which are rounded without any shine. The conure feeds on fruit and seeds, which it picks out of the fruits. They have been frequently imported and quite often bred in captivity.

JANDAYA CONURE (*Aratinga jandaya*)

Coloration: this very well known species has a golden yellow head with small red feathers. The throat area is also yellow. Breast and belly are a beautiful deep red, the back and wings green. Some of the wing feathers are blue. Rump red; tail green with yellow shine, margined with dark greenish blue. Brown eyes, black beak and grayish black feet. Females and males that have not yet reached adulthood have less red on the face and breast; some even have green spots on the breast.

Length: 30 cm.

Range: northeastern Brazil. This species inhabits primarily the young coconut tree plantations, where they do a great deal of damage. Their call is a screeching tingk-tingh-kangk. The clutch consists of two to three rounded eggs that are taken care of by the female. They feed on seeds, berries and fruits. They have been imported and bred many times. The birds become very tame and keep well in garden aviaries.

GOLDEN CONURE (*Aratinga guarouba*)

Coloration: unicolored, deep golden yellow; dark green secondaries and primaries; bill horn colored; iris brown; legs pink.

Length: 34 cm.

Range: northeastern Brazil, in rain forests. The call is shrill. The clutch consists of two to six almost rounded eggs. Their diet is composed of berries, fruits, nuts and seeds. They have been very rarely imported and not much about their wild behavior is known. Breeding reports are rare as well. This is one of the most beautiful known keel-tail parakeets.

OTHER CONURES

Twenty different species of *Pyrrhura*, which exhibit many of the characteristics of the *Aratinga* species, come from South America. Only one species populates some areas of Central America.

WHITE-EARED CONURE (*Pyrrhura leucotis*)

Coloration: the head is dark brown, as is the area around the beak and the sides of the face. This bird has a striking grayish white line by the ears and a reddish brown crown. Neck and throat are bright blue, changing to green. Black and white semicircles following the shape of the feathers run cross-wise from the throat down almost to the abdomen. The green color changes to a reddish brown marking on the belly. The tail is long and slender and brownish red. The wings are blue and green. Eyes brownish red, feet black, beak grayish black and with a yellowish white cere. The female is practically identical to the male; perhaps the colors are not as distinct.

Length: 23 cm.

Range: coastal states of Brazil and northern Venezuela.

This species populates the forests. They live together in groups that number 20-25. The clutch consists of three to nine eggs, broadly elliptically shaped. This bird feeds on seeds, fruits, nuts, berries and insects and their larvae. Although breeding results have rarely been reported, their importation frequency is fairly high.

Besides the above mentioned species, the following ones belonging to the same genus have been imported from time to time: red-eared conure (*P. hoematotis*); blue-throated conure (*P. cruentata*); maroon-bellied conure (*P. frontalis*); and the painted conure (*P. picta*).

BARRED PARAKEET (*Bolborhynchus lineola*)

Coloration: primarily green, with black shell-shaped markings on the head, neck, back, rump, and along the wings. The feathers of the wings are bordered with black. Yellow-brown eyes, gray-yellow beak and gray-black feet. The female is somewhat smaller than the male, but has the same black markings although they are smaller and less sharply defined.

Length: 16 cm.

Range: Central America from Mexico to Panama.

The birds live on oats, panicum and canary seeds, as well as fresh twigs, particularly from pear and apple trees. They are also particularly fond of various types of fruits and berries. Their song is, in contrast to that of many parakeets and parrots, not at all unpleasant.

PATAGONIAN CONURE (*Cyanoliseus patagonus*)

Coloration: Olive-brown; rump and upper tail-coverts and lower underparts yellowish-bronze; upper breast grayish-brown; grayish-white stripe along the breast; lower breast and stomach yellow; central abdomen and thighs orange-red; bill gray; iris yellowish-white; legs pink.

Length: 45 cm.

Range: mountainous regions of Chile, Argentina and Uruguay. This species populates preferably the rocky areas. Their call is a raucous screech, especially when they are flying. The female incubates the three to our eggs, which are almost spherical. This species feeds mainly on seeds, berries, fruits and such.

These birds are rarely imported. Only one couple kept in captivity has produced youngsters (England, 1964). The adults have lived with the breeder since 1960 and have been kept in a spacious outdoor aviary. A huge wooden nesting box met their demands, which was remarkable considering that these birds usually nest in holes in rocks when in the wild.

NANDAY CONURE (*Nandayus nenday*)

Coloration: primarily green. Blackish blue cap. Light green color traversed with black below the eye. Some blue on throat and upper breast. Flight feathers bluish black. Olive green tail with beautiful bluish black point; tail is very dark green underneath. Red thighs. Feet brownish pink; eyes reddish brown; bill blackish gray.

Length: 30-32 cm.

Range: South America, particularly Paraguay.

These birds are quite pleasant and can be kept in an aviary together with other species belonging to the genus *Aratinga.* They become accustomed to their owner quite quickly. I (MMV) know of a case in which a nanday conure took seed out of his owner's hand after just two weeks. Providing their accommodation is roomy, they will breed quickly. Do not hang the nesting boxes too high, because they like to sit on top of them and watch the world go by, while often making some very loud commentary.

MONK PARAKEET (*Myiopsitta monachus*)

Coloration: forehead, crown, and occiput grayish blue; cheeks, throat, and lores pale gray. Black of head, neck, rump, wing, and tail are parrot-green. The female is generally somewhat lighter in color, but in many instances there is almost no difference at all. The young birds are a brighter green initially.

Length: 30 cm.

Range: South America. A resident population introduced into southeastern New York, New Jersey and Connecticut. Nests have been recorded also from Massachusetts, Virginia and Florida.

Because of their peaceful and pleasant nature, these birds can be tamed quite readily, though their screaming may be a little loud for keeping them in the house; many times, however, their reputation for screaming proves to be exaggerated. One of the disadvantages of keeping them in an aviary is the nest that they build; although its construction is interesting enough, it takes up quite a lot of space, and they will be unlikely to breed unless their housing has very generous dimensions and shrubbery is plentiful. I (MMV) once saw a large bullet-shaped nest that had a diameter of

75 cm. Needless to say, such nest-building is fascinating. There is an entrance to the nest that is completely protected with a little portico; the parents often sit here to watch and to keep a look-out for possible danger (using it as a guard post). The nest itself consists of two rooms. The eggs are hatched in the back room, while the room that leads to the portico could be considered a living room, since the parents spend most of their time here, including the night. When the young are bigger, they, too, will move into the living room so that the female can start laying a new clutch.

The breeding season takes place mostly in October and the winter months. (Seasons given refer to those of the northern hemisphere; south of the equator seasons are reversed—January is in summer, July in winter, etc.) If possible, we should discourage winter breeding, although we know of successful cases in Holland and Belgium. However, these fanciers generally had access to heated areas in which to house their birds. Should you allow your birds to breed in the winter, you would need to provide them with extra food in the form of hard-boiled egg and white bread soaked in water or milk. This food, of course, should also be extended during their 'normal' breeding season, that is, October and November.

The female builds the nest by herself and cleans and extends it each year; it is often used for several years, perhaps even five or more. She sits on some four to eight eggs. The male does not help with these chores in the wild either. Their food requirements consist of oats, hemp (not too much!!) corn, sunflower seeds, panicum millet, canary seed, fruit, young and fresh buds and twigs, greens (lettuce, endive, chickweed, chicory, sprouts, spinach, etc.) cuttlebone and grit.

NARROW-BILLED PARAKEETS
The narrow-billed parakeet genus *Brotogeris* differs from

the other keel-tail parakeets in both appearance and behavior. They are small parrots, 18-25 cm long, of seven species and fifteen subspecies spread throughout South and Central America. A total of eight species have been imported up to this time. The bill, which gave the name to these species, is compressed sideways, the ridge is narrow, and the peak is prolonged and pointed. The tail is shorter than that of most other keel-tails, which means that it is only as long as, or even shorter than, the wings. The narrow-billed parakeets have no distinguishing sex coloration.

These birds have to be kept warm in the beginning as well as afterwards. As they are sold very often with clipped wings, they have to be kept in cages offering a variety of different branches until their wings have grown back to their original state. They can be kept in a cage, but not smaller than about 100 to 120 cm for one couple. Usually they become tame within no time, but they are bad screechers. Not many breeding successes have been reported, as breeders in general choose other species for reproduction. The birds feed on canary seeds, white and Senegal millet, spadix millet and sunflower seeds (all these in sprouted form as well) and fruit and greens. They do not nibble as much as other parakeet species, but they should always have some fresh branches available nevertheless.

CANARY-WINGED PARAKEET
(*Brotogeris versicolorus*)

Coloration: Mainly green; back and scapulars are darker; primary-coverts dark blue; inner primaries white; secondaries white with yellow; tail green above and greenish-blue below; bill grayish black with yellow tinge; iris dark brown; legs grayish-pink.

Length: 22 cm.

Range: Guyana, Brazil, southeastern Colombia and eastern Ecuador to northern Argentina. They can be seen in flocks up to many hundreds of birds. Their call is fairly loud and somewhat raucous. Their nests are termite mounds, but also in hollows of trees and such. They furnish their nest with a layer of moist moss on which they lay four to six eggs. Only the female will hatch them. The beechwood nesting boxes should be equipped with a layer of moist peatmoss. Nesting boxes should be hung as high a possible.

This is one of the most frequently imported species.

GRAY-CHEEKED PARAKEET
(*Brotogeris pyrrhopterus*)
Coloration: green: paler on underparts; forehead gray; crown bluish-green; primary-coverts dark blue; under wing-coverts orange; tail green; bill horn-colored; iris dark brown; legs pink.
Length: 20 cm.
Range: west of the Andes. They inhabit arid scrublands in the tropical zone.

Living in large flocks, they utter loud, raucous notes. The clutch of three to six eggs which are rounded have to be inclubated for approximately 32 days. They feed on fruits and seeds. This species is an extremely nice "pet" bird.

ORANGE-CHINNED PARAKEET
(*Brotogeris jugularis*)
Coloration: green; lower parts more yellowish; orange chin; lower back and rump with blue; wing-coverts olive-brown; thighs and under tail-coverts green with a bluish tinge; bill gray-black; iris, dark brown; legs light brown.
Length: 18 cm.
Range: southwestern Mexico, south to northern Colombia and northern Venezuela.

In the wild this species lives together in small troops (10-20) in the woods (though they will go up to approximately 1000 meters above sea level in the mountains), where they look for fruit, soft leaf buds, twigs and berries. The young are raised in large part on soft fruit. They are fond of insects. Their clutch consisting of about four round eggs which are laid in holes or termite mounds. This species has frequently been imported.

TUI PARAKEET (*Brotogeris sanctithomae*)
Coloration: green, paler and more yellow on the underside; bluish on cheeks and nape; forehead, lores and forecrown yellow; primaries dark green, bill brownish; iris gray; legs pale grayish-brown.
Length: 17 cm.
Range: western Brazil, Peru, Lower Amazon, and Ecuador. In the wild the nest is usually built about 5 meters from the ground, well hidden between branches and leaves. I (MMV) was personally able to witness in 1969 some nests made in termite hills (Peru). The female lays four to six eggs. A roomy beechwood nesting box would be ideal. This smallest species of its genus has been imported quite often.

RINGNECKED PARAKEETS

ALEXANDRINE PARAKEET (*Psittacula eupatria*)
Coloration: green, back of the head and cheeks greenish. Clearly visible collar and cheek markings. The collar, red. Innermost tail feathers are bluish green with yellow-white tips. Gray eyes, encircled with red; deep red bill and grayish brown feet. The female is very similar to the male; however, she lacks the bands on the collar and cheeks.
Length: 58 cm.
Range: Ceylon, eastern Afghanistan and western Pakistan through India to Indochina; on the Andaman Islands. They are inhabitants of the lowlands and coastal areas, preferring mangroves.
Their call is loud. Clutches consist of two to four eggs

The canary-winged parakeet, *Brotogeris versicolorus chiriri*, is small and slender, but is shaped like a standard parrot rather than a parakeet.

The Malabar
parakeet, *Psittacula
columboides,* is rare
in its native
southwestern India.
Females have black
bills and lack the col-
lar.

which are laid on a layer of decayed wood. The birds feed besides the basic nourishment on nuts, blossoms, leaf buds and nectar. The natives are annoyed by the birds' wasteful feeding habits.

ROSE-RINGED PARAKEET (*Psittacula krameri*)

Coloration: green with a black collar and a black band around the bill. Behind the black collar there is a red shine. Belly and under tail-coverts are yellowish green. Uppermost tail feathers are bluish-green with yellow tips. Iris yellow-orange, beak red, and feet black. The female lacks the black collar and the red glow behind the collar. Young birds take their time in achieving their true colors (2 years).

Length: 40 cm.

Range: Central and northeastern Africa, Afghanistan, West Pakistan through India, and Nepal to Burma and Sri Lanka. They inhabit timbered areas, farmlands and the vicinity of habitations, as well as woodlands. Their call is very loud. They have a variable breeding season and find their nesting facilities in a hollow trunk or a high tree. The clutch has two to six eggs. The birds feed on blossoms and nectar in addition to the basic foods.

PLUM-HEADED PARAKEET
(*Psittacula cyanocephala*)

Coloration: the male has a plum-colored head and wings; black seam around the head, followed by a bluish green band. Dark green wings. Balance of body is light green. Innermost tail feathers bluish green, outer tail feathers green with light yellow tips. Brown eyes, yellowish white bill; grayish brown feet. The head of the female is considerably lighter, and the red shoulder marking is missing. Her head is grayish purple. Young birds reach their adult colors after a full two years. Since young males look like females before these two years have elapsed, we need to be very careful when purchasing these birds.

Range: Sri Lanka, Rameswaram Island, India, West Pakistan and Nepal. They are commonly inhabitants of hills, jungles and cultivated areas. They can cause quite a lot of damage.

Their call can vary in fairly melodious notes. Several birds may nest in holes in the same tree. The clutch consists of four to six spherical, non-glossy eggs. This species feeds on seeds, fruits, nuts, blossoms and leaf buds; it is easy to breed and has been imported very frequently.

AUSTRALIAN PARAKEETS

As Australian parakeets are easy to keep and as they show a great deal of pleasant and friendly characteristics, they are very much favored as aviary birds. All the different species are very nice to look at. Their demands are minimal as regards feeding material and keeping facilities. Quite a few different species have been bred. One of their species, the budgerigar, is the most popular house pet (right after the canary) bird species throughout the entire pet-keeping world. They can be kept together with every other small bird but never with another parrot. Unlike most parakeets they do not screech but chatter pleasantly during the day. Their size ranges from about 40 cm, to about 22 cm.

All of the Australian parakeets are most comfortable when kept in outdoor aviaries. The aviary should not be less than 5 meters in length for the bigger species and not less than 2½ meters for smaller ones. All species need a shelter room, which should be draft-free and heatable if possible; the shelter should be dry and have some kind of light. Some of the species will certainly die if they have to stay at freezing temperatures.

All species have to be fed canary seeds, white and Senegal millet. As supplemental foods they take sunflower seeds and oats, of which the smaller species should not get too much; especially the hemp portions should be rationed, as it is too rich and greasy. During this period the parents

1

2

3

4

5

6

7

8

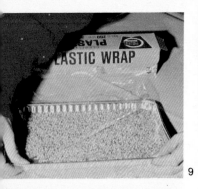

SEED GERMINATION requires any birdseed which is fresh. You also require (1) an aluminum tray, a strainer, bowl, and plastic wrap. The strainer must fit into the bowl and be able to support itself (2) on the rim. Fill the strainer with the birdseed (3), and rinse it under running water until it is thoroughly clean (4). Allow it to soak for about a day (5) in the bowl. Change the water as frequently as convenient, but at least once every 12 hours. Then pour the dampened seed into the tray (6) and spread the seed uniformly (7). Mix in any mold-inhibiting substance (Moldex) and cover the seed to keep the moisture in, but not to stop air from getting to the seed (8, 9). If you want to grow *grass* from the seed you can use earth (10), sprinkle it with seed (11), mix the seed with the earth (12), sprinkle lightly with water (13) and store in a warm, dark place (14). The seed used with earth can either be soaked for a while (see above 1 through 5), or straight from the box.

have to be fed sufficiently with very nourishing food like hemp, unroasted peanuts to the larger ones, spadix mix for the tiny species. Moreover, you should see that they get some sprouted seeds, greens like chickweed, panicle-grass, lettuce, spinach and endive salad. Some of the different species do not particularly like the greens, but almost all of them are fond of the sprouted seeds. It is no problem to get them used to taking sweet fruits like apples, pears, oranges and grapes.

RED-WINGED PARAKEET
(*Aprosmictus erythropterus*)

Coloration: the male has a green head, neck and flight feathers. Dark green back, light blue rump, flowing into green-yellow. Green tail, edged in yellow. Light yellow-green underside, or yellow with green glow. Wing-coverts are red. Yellow-green flanks; black 'cloak' feathers. Upper tail-coverts are light greenish brown and yellow-green. Brown eyes; red bill with black band; grayish brown feet. The female is green without much gloss. A small amount of red along the edge of the wing. Offspring resemble the female, though the iris is black initially and later red. At one and a half years of age the males can be distinguished from the female by the black in their feathers.

Length: 32 cm.

Range: Northern and northeastern Australia and southern New Guinea.

Flocks up to 20 birds populate the wooded savannah along the coasts. Their call sounds sharp and metallic. Besides the basic materials they feed on nuts, blossoms, nectar, insects and insect larvae. They love eucalyptus and acacia seeds and mistletoe berries. The eggs are laid in deeply hollowed limbs or tree holes near the water. The clutch consists of three to six rounded eggs. Although the Australian species are usually easier to breed, most imports have been effected from New Guinea.

Polytelis parakeets are represented by three species, all of which have been imported. They are very seldom seen to be kept nowadays, as their supply entirely depends on domestic breeders' results.

Polytelis parakeets have an elegantly shaped body. Their tail is elongated and becomes slimmer towards the end. The two middle feathers are the longest. These species can get very tame yet always will stay very active. As they are very talented flyers, the aviary has to be spacious enough for them; six meters of length is the minimum. In such an aviary it is no problem to keep them together with smaller birds, although the best thing is always to keep parakeets separately from the others, as some of them are reliable breeders.

They are fairly resistant against cold but should always have a shelter room which is frostfree at their disposal, especially during nighttime. Their main food has to consist of canary seeds, millet and sunflower seeds, oats and a little hemp. While feeding their young ones they should get some peanuts, sprouted seeds, greens and fruit daily.

SUPERB PARAKEET (*Polytelis swainsonii*)

Coloration: the male is green, bright light yellow forehead, throat, and cheeks. Red blotch on the throat. Flight feathers are blue; the lovely tail is green, margined in blue; underside of the tail is black. Orange-yellow eyes. Red bill, brown feet. The green coloring of the hen is less sharp than that of the male. No yellow on the head. Thighs show some red feathers. Some pink underneath the tail. Brown eyes.

Length: 40 cm.

Range: Australia: mainly along the Murray and Murrumbidgee Rivers in New South Wales and bordering regions, including the deep northern areas of Victoria and stretching out to above the Castlereagh River and the Lanchlan River, even to the east of Sydney. This area is the smallest territory of any of the Australian flat-tailed birds.

Left: This orange-fronted conure, *Aratinga canicularis clarae*, comes from western Mexico and is a popular pet in the United States. It is almost always sold as a "dwarf parrot" and is quite reasonable in cost. Above: The Queen of Bavaria conure, *Aratinga guarouba*, is from northwestern Brazil and is also called the golden or yellow conure. The length is slightly over fourteen inches. It is large and heavy bodied.

REGENT PARAKEET (*Polytelis anthopeplus*)

Coloration: the male is yellowish green. Grass-green back with dark markings. The wings are yellow with black flight feathers and black wing curves. Wing-coverts are red, margined in yellow. Tail black with a blue shine, deep black on underside. Red eyes and beak; grayish brown feet. Where the male is yellow (or yellow-green) the female is green. Red stripes on the tail. Deep dark green on top side of tail. Young birds resemble the female. After about six months the males will start to color up, and after eighteen months they will have achieved adult coloring.

Length: 35-40 cm.

Range: Australia; northern parts of Victoria and bordering areas of New South Wales to the low eucalyptus growth areas of southeastern South Australia. They are also found in southwestern Australia to the east of Esperance.

A noteworthy fact about these birds is that the young have black eyes until the first molting, which takes place at around eighteen months of age; after that the eyes are red.

Regent parakeets are very pleasantly natured birds that are regularly offered for sale on the market. They are even pleasant toward small exotic species such as red-eared waxbills, zebra finches and fire finches. They might prove to be less tolerant toward fellow species particularly if they are housed in a somewhat small aviary and during the breeding period.

PRINCESS PARAKEET (*Polytelis alexandrae*)

Coloration: male: crown and area around the eye are a vague sea-blue. Yellow/gray/green at the back of the head and neck, shoulders, and back. Throat, breast and parts of the cheeks are pinkish red. Bright sky blue rump. Pinkish red feathers around the feet. Light yellow-green on the underside and wings; flight feathers are white. Light orange eyes, encircled with red (not in the female); red bill, brown feet. The blue in the female is grayish blue, particularly the center feathers of the tail, but often the entire tail is shorter and deep red on the inside, margined in black. Bill is not as red as in the male; there is less violet on the rump.

Not until they are six months old do they start to show differences that will enable the determination of their sex. The eyes will give the first indication, followed by a bluish haze on the head of the males.

Length: 35-36½ cm.

Range: the deep inland areas of Australia, from the central western and northwestern regions to the northern parts of South Australia.

Their nesting behavior is similar to that of the above two species. Their eggs are rounded and glossy. Their main diet is seed, which they find on the ground. This species belongs to one of the most beautiful parakeets available on the pet market.

THE ROSELLAS

The rosella group (genus *Platycercus*) includes six species, of which five have their place of origin in Australia and one in Tasmania and on the islands of Bass Strait. Some of them vary only slightly from each other, whereas others are different enough to have been named as different species in former times. As all of them have a very close relationship with each other, they often cross-breed in the areas where their territories overlap; the matings are fertile. A very particular characteristic for *Platycercus* species is the scale-design along the back feathers. A black center point is edged in yellow, red or green. All species show a big spot on their cheeks colored in white, yellow or blue. The tail feathers are comparatively broad; the four middle ones reach almost the same length. The beak is short and powerful. The two sexes are colored almost the same which makes it very difficult to differentiate them. In only one species is there sexual dimorphism.

The rose-ringed parakeet, *Psittacula krameri*, has the most extensive range of any parrot. Different subspecies are found in Africa
and India, which is the basis for calling the birds Indian or African

ringnecks. A popular favorite, this bird is widely kept and frequently bred in captivity. Wild-caught individuals continue to be available, as the rose-ringed is sufficiently abundant to be considered a pest in some areas.

All of the rosella species are very popular, as they are very resistant to cold and diseases. They are active and very skillful flyers, so they need an aviary of at least 5 meters. Most of them are reliable breeders once they have accepted each other, so it is not advisable to bring a new female to a freshly widowed male, as usually he will chase her to death. The best thing is to bring them together after a certain period of time near each other by keeping them one beside the other in small cages. Another help would be to place the male in a different aviary. As rosellas alway react very aggressively against fellow species, they should never be kept together or in adjoining aviaries, as they tend to hurt themselves by biting each other through the wire netting. Direct contact with close relatives like grass parakeets should be avoided, whereas no aggressive incidents have been reported between rosellas and other small species.

The nesting needs of rosellas are not very special apart from the fact that they need a spacious nest. The clutch can number up to nine eggs. The brooding time is 18 to 20 days, and the young ones leave their nest relatively early at the age of 30 to 35 days. They reach their independence after one month and should be separated from their parents, as these very often are about to undergo a second brooding period.

The feeding process does not reveal any difficulty. They simply feed on canary seeds, white Senegal and Japanese millet, oats, wheat and sunflower seeds, from time to time some peanuts and a little hemp. They love spadix millet, especially sprouted, as do all other parakeet species. It is good to offer as many sprouted seeds as well as greens and fruit as the birds can possibly eat every day.

As all exportation is prohibited by the Australian government, breeders should always try to keep the different species from cross-breeding and thus from the certain extinction of several species originating in Australia.

EASTERN ROSELLA (*Platycercus eximius*)

Coloration: sexes are almost alike in plumage; head and breast red; white cheek spots; breast yellow running into faded green on abdomen; under tail-coverts red; back and wings black bordered; outer flight wings blue; middle tail feathers faded green with a touch of blue; lateral ones faded blue with white specks; bill grayish-white; iris dark brown; legs gray.

Length: 30 cm.

Range: southeastern Australia.

This species spends most of its time in the treetops feeding on seeds and blossoms, uttering a loud metallic piping with their high-pitched voice. The clutch of four to seven, sometimes even nine, rounded eggs keep the parents busy for many months, as the birds acquire independence only comparatively late. This species is easy to keep in captivity and is recommended for novices, as it is extremely willing to breed.

PALE-HEADED ROSELLA (*Platycercus adscitus*)

Coloration: no obvious distinguishing points for the sexes; head white; cheek spots violet-blue, upper part of the spots whitish; breast yellow, lower part and abdomen blue; vent and under tail-coverts red; wing-coverts black; outer flight-coverts blue; tail feathers green with a touch of blue and lateral ones pale blue tipped with white; bill horn-colored; iris dark brown; legs gray.

Length: 30 cm.

Range: northeastern Australia. This bird inhabits timbered country and clearings in forests as well as adjoining open grassland.

The call is similar to the one of the eastern rosella. The nest is in a deep hollow of trees near the water. The clutch consists of three to five rounded eggs. Because of their partiality to cultivations of cereal and maize crops and or-

77

Left: The African ringneck or rose-ringed parakeet, *Psittacula k. krameri,* is slightly smaller than the Indian ringneck. Young birds take a long time to mature. At least a two-year wait is necessary to determine sex. Some do not mature until they are three years old. Above: The Alexandrine parakeet, *Psittacula eupatria nipalensis,* has a large head and a huge bill that seem out of proportion. All in all, it appears to be a gross caricature of the ringneck.

79

chards, they sometimes become a pest when living in numbers.

WESTERN ROSELLA (*Platycercus icterotis*)

Coloration: the only rosella species with sexual dimorphism conspicuously developed. Male: head and underparts red; yellow cheek spots; back and wings black bordered, dark green colored; rump and central tail feathers green; wing-coverts black; flight feathers outwardly blue; lateral tail feathers pale blue tipped with white; bill gray; iris dark brown; legs brownish-gray; Female: green with red and yellow; lower underparts red, frontal band red.

Length: 25 cm.

Range: southwestern Australia. They live in open forests, grasslands and cultivated farmlands.

The call is melodious, which makes them different in one more point from the other members of the genus.

The clutch consisting of about five eggs is laid in the hollow of a eucalyptus tree and has to be incubated for 25 days. The diet consists of grass seeds and such, fruits, berries and insects and the like.

GENUS BARNARDIUS

The ringneck parakeets (genus *Barnardius*) are very similar to the *Platycercus* species. Some scientists even place them in the same genus (*see Checklist of Birds of the World,* by Peters) and others try to explain the differentiation points of their cranium bones and feather coloration as well as behavior. As both genera are very similar to each other, cross-breeding occurs where their territories overlap.

In captivity ringneck parakeets keep their similarity to the rosella species. They are not very sensitive to cold temperatures and can be kept in outdoor aviaries all year long. Both groups are quarrelsome against other parakeet species. Although some of the ringnecks are good breeders, they generally give more problems than rosellas until they decide to mate. Their food demands are the same.

Barnardius species are difficult to sex. It is the similarity in coloration which is extremely annoying. Moreover, the different species have a wide range of coloration in itself. Generally the males are somewhat bigger than the females; their heads and beaks are especially stronger.

MALLEE RINGNECK PARAKEET
(*Barnardius barnardi*)

Coloration: sex differentiation is extremely difficult; crown and nape green; frontal band red; bluish cheek spots; yellow collar around hindneck; underparts turquoise; orange-yellow band running irregularly across abdomen; back deep dark blue; median wing-coverts yellow; rump green, wings green; central tail-feathers green with blue markings; lateral ones pale blue; bill grayish-white; iris dark brown; legs gray.

Length: 33 cm.

Range: interior of southern Queensland, western New South Wales, northwestern Victoria and eastern part of Southern Australia, west to the York Peninsula. Three subspecies generally populate wooded country close to water. They spend most of the day on the ground searching for seeds, small insects, etc. The nest in a hollow limb or hole in a tree is lined with decayed wood dust on the bottom of the cavity. Normally the clutch contains four to six rounded eggs. Besides the basic diet, the birds feed on blossoms, leaf buds, insects and their larvae.

PORT LINCOLN PARAKEET (*Barnardius zonarius*)

Coloration: Head black; lower ear-coverts violet-blue; thin yellow collar around hindneck; back, wings and rump brilliant green; under wing-coverts blue; throat and breast bluish-green; belly yellow; under tail-coverts yellowish-green; tail feathers dark green with blue markings, the

4

1. Indian ring-necked parakeet, *Psittacula krameri manillensis*. 2, 4, 5. Indian ring-necked parakeet, lutino color variety bred in captivity. 3. Plum-headed parakeet, *P. c. cyanocephala.* This beautiful bird is very tolerant towards other parakeets, even towards little finches, although for breeding purposes a pair should be given a large garden aviary to themselves.

5

lateral ones faded blue with white spots; bill grayish horn-colored; iris brown; legs gray.

Length: 38 cm.

Range: central and western Australia. This species is divided into three subspecies, generally found populating the dense coastal forests, the semi-arid eucalyptus-dominated wheatbelt and the arid scrublands (Forshaw). They communicate in almost the same way as the above-mentioned species, yet their voice has a somewhat higher sound. Their nesting habits are similar. Since their territory covers an enormous area, it is unlikely that they will become extinct, though some caution should be exercised; their numbers have decreased over the last hundred years, particularly due to the fact that many of them are shot by farmers because of the destruction they wreak in orchards and cornfields.

GENUS *PSEPHOTUS*

The genus *Psephotus* contains five different species, two of which are often found in aviaries. The remaining three species are rarely found out of their natural environment.

These parakeets are comparatively small. Their wings are sometimes as long as their tails, sometimes even longer. The coloration of the sexes is different, which helps the breeders to get their couples together. Birds of this genus have a pleasant voice and never screech. The two commonly bred species are comparatively insensitive to cold weather conditions but should be kept in a sheltered room during night time.

Food needs are canary seeds and a millet assortment, all of which should be given as sprouted products as well. Oats and wheat should be sprouted only before offering. The sunflower seeds and hemp have to be sparingly rationed, but greens and fruit should alway be available for the birds.

Together with the budgerigar and the cockatiel, these parakeets belong to the most commonly kept birds in captivity. As they are reliable and easy to breed, the pet market demand can be satisfied completely by domestically bred species. Although these parakeets are very moderate in their needs, the aviary should not be less than 3 meters in length. The clutch, usually consisting of four to seven eggs, will need about 20 days to hatch; the young ones leave the nest after 30 to 35 days, and the parents will continue to feed them for another couple of days. It is important to separate them as soon as the old ones start to chase their children, as this means that they have to get ready for a new breeding period. Even though they easily could have several breeding periods during one season, the birds should not be allowed to bring up more than two clutches per year.

As *Psephotus* parents are very reliable in their caring tasks, they make good foster parents.

RED-RUMPED PARAKEET
(*Psephotus haematonotus*)

Coloration: sexual dimorphism is pronounce. Males: generally green; wings and back more bluish; abdomen yellow; vents and under tail-coverts white; rump red; median wing-coverts yellow; under ones and outer part of primaries blue; bill black; iris dark brown; legs gray.

Length: 27 cm.

Range: interior of southeastern Australia. This species is divided into two subspecies. They live in lightly timbered grasslands, open plains and cultivated farmlands.

The call sounds like a whistle. A clutch consists generally of four to seven eggs which are rounded. Both male and female conduct an intensive search, sometimes taking days, for a suitable nesting place. They generally will choose a hollow in thick branches or in the trunks of trees, including dead trees. These parakeets feed on grass seeds and such and greens, particularly the leaves of various thistles, chickweed, etc. They belong to the most commonly kept species in captivity and are not difficult to breed.

1. The Australian king parakeet, *Alisterus s. scapularis,* is the most majestic of all the parakeets. 2. The Stanley rosella, *Platycercus i. icterotis,* is the smallest of the rosellas and is the only rosella in which the sexes have a different coloration. 3. The crimson winged parakeet, *Aprosmictus e. erythropterus,* inhabits eastern Australia from southern Queensland to New South Wales. 4. The golden-mantled rosella, *Platycercus eximius cecilae,* inhabits the same area as the crimson winged parakeet. All of the mantle feathers have bright yellow margins, hence the name.

87

GRASS PARAKEETS

The grass parakeets (genus *Neophema*) include seven species, five of which are more or less popular in our aviaries. In general, grass parakeets are perfectly qualified to get accustomed to aviary conditions. They are beautiful and peaceful and do not screech or destroy wood, and they breed frequently and reliably. They just need a spacious cage to be happy. If breeding is required, a pair can live in a cage of 2½ to 3 meters in length. An aviary of the above mentioned size can easily house a pair of grass parakeets together with three pairs of *Polytelis* species, as the grass parakeets never get attacked by the *Polytelis* species. But they should never have to live together with other parakeet species, as there will always be competition among them.

As grass parakeets are sensitive to cold and especially to humidity, they should be kept in a slightly heated room during the cold season, even if some breeders keep them successfully outside all year long. Unlike other Australian parakeet species, grass parakeets seem to get along pretty well and even breed inside the house. They need to be fed just like song parakeets but should be kept from too much hemp as well as too many sunflower seeds. It is advisable to add some eggfood for young ones.

The clutch consists of four to six eggs, which take about 18 days until they hatch. The young birds leave their nest about 30 to 35 days later and should be removed to another cage after three weeks, as the parents start a new breeding period. Never allow more than two breeding periods per year.

Grass parakeets are extremely sensitive to dirt; they respond to dirty cages with eye inflammations, so their homes should always be kept utterly neat.

As all the specimens offered on today's market are generally domestically bred ones, they are not so delicate any more. Still, they have to be kept in clean and spacious cages and provided with good food and draft-free shelters.

A problem with grass parakeets is that they tend to panic, especially during the night. They easily get started and fly against the wire netting or the roof of the aviary, damaging their delicate cranium bones. This habit is easy to be overcome by keeping them in a slightly lighted shelter room during the night.

ELEGANT PARAKEET (*Neophema elegans*)

Coloration: the male is golden yellow; lighter on the underside of the tail. Yellow triangle between bill and eyes. Small blue eyebrow. Blue edges on the wing feathers. Some orange feathers on the lower belly. Olive-green back. Black flight feathers. The female is less vivid yellow; no orange feathers on the belly (although some females may have these; they usually disappear, however, after one or two molts). Blue flight feathers. Young males are a brighter yellow than the females at the time they leave the nest, but do not yet have the band on the forehead. After six months, the juvenile molting is finished.

Length: 23 cm.

Range: southern portion of New South Wales, western Victoria, south Australia (north to Flinders Ranges) and southwestern Australia (north to Moora and east to Esperance).

This species, which lives in pairs or in small groups, is considered one of the most common of the *Neophema* representatives. It can often be found not too far away from civilization and has even been found on the northern border of Western Australia, in the Pilbara District, which is in the tropics!! The birds live near woods, though not in them, on open grass terrain and new plantations; it would almost seem as if they avoid trees. Many of them live along the coast, where we saw them several times early in the morning, flying high up in the sky.

Their nests are found in hollow trees, usually 1 to 2 meters above the ground. The clutch consists of four to five

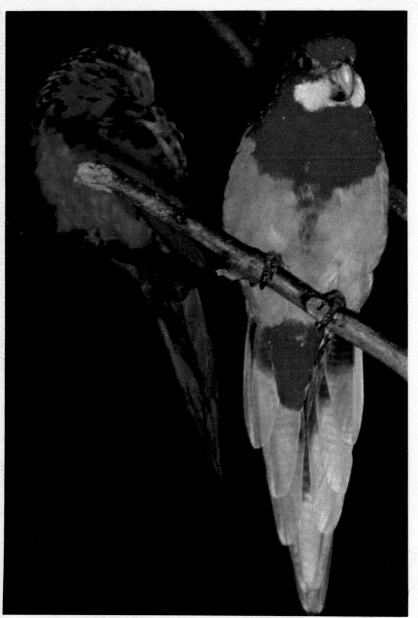

Left: The blue or mealy rosella, *Platycercus a. adsitcus,* is an ideal aviary bird, but should be kept by themselves because of their aggressiveness toward other birds. Above: The golden-mantled rosella, *P. eximius cecilae,* also has a reputation for aggressiveness with other parrot-like birds, although it is one of the most popular and most beautiful parakeets in aviculture.

rounded eggs. This species is the favorite one to be kept in captivity, as the other *Neophema* species give much more trouble by their choosiness and delicate nature. This explains why they are not always available on the pet market.

BUDGERIGAR (*Melopsittacus undulatus*) and COCKATIEL (*Nymphicus hollandicus*)

No book dealing with dwarf parrots or parakeets would be complete without sufficient reference to two of the most popular birds in the world, the Australian shell parakeet, also called the budgerigar, and the cockatiel (also found in Australia). But so many books have been written about these two birds . . . and so much is known about their breeding, training, care, color varieties and genetics . . . that it would take more pages than are available to even discuss these points in any sensible detail.

If you are interested in these two parrots you should buy a book dealing specifically with the bird you have selected. The care of these two species is simpler than that of any other bird mentioned in this book.

T.F.H. Publications, publisher of this book, has published specific books on these two birds. They are available wherever you bought this book.

Left: Cockatiels are considered to be among the best of all easily reared birds. Right: The evident good health of this budgie is a result not only of providing the right food, but also of feeding the best quality foods available.